NOT THE TIME FOR DRAGON SLAYING

ZACK MOY

Put here on
Mar 18 2018
17th St Community Bookst

Dear Diary Series, Vol. I

zackmoy.com

Cover Art by Chas Barton
Instagram: @fool.official

ISBN: 1978282826
ISBN-13: 978-1978282827

For Alex —

keep chasing the dream

Dear Diary Series, Vol. I

April - September 2017

"Nobody will stop you from creating. Do it tonight. Do it tomorrow. That is the way to make your soul grow – whether there is a market for it or not! The kick of creation is the act of creating, not anything that happens afterward. I would tell all of you... before you go to bed, write a four line poem. Make it as good as you can. Don't show it to anybody. Put it where nobody will find it. And you will discover that you have your reward."

—Kurt Vonnegut

I was never any good at following all the instructions.

APRIL 1ST

To go somewhere has nothing
to do with moving.
We can't go anywhere if
we're not in the same place.

APRIL 2ND

It always seems to happen.
In an airport bathroom
right after eating
asparagus.

APRIL 3RD

Too much of a good thing–
it's why sunshine burns.
"I'm still gonna eat
the whole fucking pint."

APRIL 4TH

Stuffy nose sinus headache sore throat
crippling depression:
sometimes the best medicine is falling
flat on your face.

APRIL 5TH

I believe late is
better than never but
the truth is exhausting:
I'm running out of time

APRIL 6TH

"Take a break & stop moving,
you need to just relax…"
Being still doesn't mean
being idle.

APRIL 7TH

Friends in my "inner circle"
will confess it's a boxing match
where I throw nothing but
compliments & panic attacks.

APRIL 8TH

Has anyone ever told you?
How you're unexpectedly
sweet
like cavities.

APRIL 9TH

I love how you text me
an hour before we meet
to tell me, “Hey,
I can’t make it tonight.”

APRIL 10TH

I can't trust the Spring
when the oceans are
still black and blue.
Even Fall's head goes grey.

APRIL 11TH

i’ve been packing my bags
looking at sunday
waiting for someday
when my house isn’t haunted

APRIL 12TH

And the Lord said unto
his followers, "like and be shared!"
For he who is social is
wiser and woke.

APRIL 13TH

The ultimate constraint
bears more than it scares—
scares us into the damnedest things;
I'm dedicating every day to you

APRIL 14TH

swear to me (when i die)
no promise me
you won't serve me
on the rocks

APRIL 15TH

The green warlock cast a spell,
his illuminating incantation
faber est suae quisque fortunae
conjured 529s and backdoor Roths.

APRIL 16TH

“disruption” is polite
 euphemism
 an abbreviated form of
“my problem, now all theirs”

APRIL 17TH

Insomnia is your friend
who just started improv
and can't shut the fuck up
about the question game?

APRIL 18TH

She proclaimed, "Tomorrow
we erase the memory of their legacy.
To die forgotten is to never exist.
To be regretted."

APRIL 19TH

they tell me smell is the strongest
memory trigger
but you always tasted like
a sad memory to me

APRIL 20TH

No matter what you do
to the seeds,
grass never grows
up tangled by itself

APRIL 21ST

where were you
when you went missing?
we are all we
look for

APRIL 22ND

Melancholy is anger
stuck on mute
and you swear to God
the remote is invisible.

APRIL 23RD

"But we all look the same
with the lights off?'—
pillow-whispers as she tiptoes
to turn them back on.

APRIL 24TH

(What I won't tell you)
If I scream quietly enough
I can step outside
myself

APRIL 25TH

"Make mistakes,"
 he said… clarifying,
"But don't be
 the mistakes that made you."

APRIL 26TH

We twentysomethings
shouldn't be getting
too old for this shit.
I think we can do better.

APRIL 27TH

On Monday just after noon
there were reports of gunfire
after the suspect allegedly
spoiled yesterday's Game of Thrones

APRIL 28TH

looking for hope
hoping to help
anxious when it's time
as I lay waiting for patience

APRIL 29TH

Raise a glass
to my dear friends hailing from
Scotland Japan and Kentucky
I wish I didn't have

APRIL 30TH

It's hard being half a world
away but even harder standing
right next to each other
traveling in opposite directions

MAY 1ST

No amount of coffee
can cure the exhaustion
after a day with your mother.
(Yawn on behalf of my eyebags.)

MAY 2ND

Swiping right through headlines
without reading between the lines.
Who can you look up to
when you're always looking down?

MAY 3RD

Don't take it personally
when she crosses her arms.
She is not fancy.
She just wears black.

MAY 4TH

scattered paint chips
rusting gears & their chain
muddy handlebar tassels that
still lust for wind

MAY 5TH

He finishes his drink mumbling,
“stirred, never shaken,
I’d rather be a single, neat
than a double, on the rocks.”

MAY 6TH

Sometimes you're the sturdiest
umbrella in an expected downpour,
only to be forgotten
at home

MAY 7TH

familiar phrasing from a
forgotten phone number.
memory don’t work like
shedding skin.

MAY 8TH

remember
to look both ways
before stepping outside
your shadow

MAY 9TH

on dark nights the bottom
of your sink begs for
leaks despite hating
rust

MAY 10TH

Sand yourself
down to your rough edges
until you belong like
worn fabric

MAY 11TH

Don't call me darling.
You'll see your
blindspots
same as I soon enough.

MAY 12TH

Picture of a
picture.
When I grow up I wanna be
derivative.

MAY 13TH

some homes
pine for rain and
emergency entrances.
others only rain.

MAY 14TH

Smelling yourself
is the best way to know
who you were
last night

MAY 15TH

There's charm to being
lost.
(Wondering whether
they're looking)

MAY 16TH

tempo always
rushes in
the march of life.
every step is funeral.

MAY 17TH

A rough draft in red ink
A moment of truth at dusk
A movement stretching you
out of your goddamn mind

MAY 18TH

your ultraviolet smile
leaves my skin peeling
but i'm learning that
burning starts the healing

MAY 19TH

change the scenery
if the shimmer fizzles.
home is where the
endgame is.

MAY 20TH

someone showing their teeth
behind a red X
above bold words
NO JOKING PLEASE

MAY 21ST

no medals awarded
after 26 miles
and collapsing
300m from the finish

MAY 22ND

The scariest dream
I ever had is
the one
that came true

MAY 23RD

When the Sun's in the sky
it's always shining it's always
burning it's always full.
Don't be somebody's Moon.

MAY 24TH

This is not what I had in mind
when I jumped off
the edge.
(There's nothing down here.)

MAY 25TH

Mama always said to leave
the campsite cleaner than
we found it,
but our definitions differ.

MAY 26TH

If butterflies wear yoga pants
is their meditation more mindful?
Do they remember their wingless past?
Can you think so much you forget?

MAY 27TH

If you discover a shell that sings
remember to actually listen.
The best gifts the sea gives
are its lyrics.

MAY 28TH

Give me a minute.
I need to stretch
out after all these
calories.

MAY 29TH

Little did he know,
the green grape would grow
up strong, age quickly, and give
a young crush the courage

MAY 30TH

I'd hate to be an Olympian
in the Cretaceous period
on team T. rex
swimming the breaststroke

MAY 31ST

I don't miss you
making me smile head-to-toe,
only the moment after, sore-abbed,
and the way I suddenly saw myself

JUNE 1ST

The lowest leaves on the tree
may receive the brightest rays,
but if you listen closely
you'll still only hear the wind.

JUNE 2ND

Sneaking incognito
down a dark alley
unable to hear your own footsteps:
you've already lost yourself.

JUNE 3RD

Stay close, little one.
The night is almost over —
we'll finally see
the monsters' faces.

JUNE 4TH

Here comes Chuck Norris!
storming in on his steed,
prepared to save us from
the hand that feeds

JUNE 5TH

I always tried to make
the sand climb up the glass,
but I've accepted
I can't make minutes.

JUNE 6TH

A game they used to play
when they were younger:
kiss everywhere
except the mouth

JUNE 7TH

Are we still here?
You're taking too long
to change.
I got my shoes on now.

JUNE 8TH

Even unimaginable pain
looks pleasurable
when you're smitten.
Just don't take off your glasses.

JUNE 9TH

Ankles strained. Hamstring torn.
The rubber on her soles is nearly gone.
She's been running for days
away from her future.

JUNE 10TH

He lost his why in the garage
but on the street found a how.
Everything is lost and found
and only for now.

JUNE 11TH

It's easy to surf
if you're riding a wave.
Even easier is simply
drifting away

JUNE 12TH

Here she is
posing for a full length mirror
in a red cocktail dress,
unable to scream

JUNE 13TH

The first test
in a new relationship:
the first fart.
Did I pass?

JUNE 14TH

There is a light in your eyes
whose color I'd forgotten.
I'm afraid.
I'm afraid I'll burn it out.

JUNE 15TH

The summer breeze
reminds me I am covered
in tiny hairs and
the world is frigid

JUNE 16TH

"Live for that lived-in quality!"
Do you look for better?
Even the cockroach looks for
something better.

JUNE 17TH

no one
deserves to be forgotten
but you and I —
we're not that special

JUNE 18TH

I spent an afternoon
selling solutions to capitalism.
I left with nothing except
warm ale and tall shadows.

JUNE 19TH

a barrel to the head
nobody comes or goes when
he holds his liquor
hostage

JUNE 20TH

Thought they were a pair but
he was Lego and
he was K'nex and
force only holds together so long

JUNE 21ST

Respect the rock pusher
all you want
but if that's not your punishment
there's no need to suffer

JUNE 22ND

The human body must have a sense
of humor
when it willingly makes itself
sick

JUNE 23RD

The red wheelbarrow
rolling in the red barn
under the scorching red sun.
Yes, this is the insistence of sex.

JUNE 24TH

The quietest place
I've ever visited
is a public park
after a Pride parade

JUNE 25TH

we're all a phone call away
from facing that truth
we've been trying to
screen for years

JUNE 26TH

It's not that
I find you boring,
our talks just trigger
my narcolepsy

JUNE 27TH

Feed your food
with the freshest attention.
Your deepest hungers
will calm.

JUNE 28TH

Collections are the dust bunnies
who grow into armies
destined for coups
hopping all over you

JUNE 29TH

I keep having this damn nightmare
where a stranger confesses to me
I'm memorable but not
remarkable

JUNE 30TH

Two years from 30
and all I want on the weekend
is to setup a play date
with myself

JULY 1ST

The night you passed the Bar
we fell asleep in the tub.
Those blankets sure helped, but
your shoulders are still bony.

JULY 2ND

So close to fortune is enough
to make a man forget how to dance.
Focus on your circumstance.
I'm trending towards staggering stumbling

JULY 3RD

What happens if you join the 27 Club?
Does Amy lead blessings on Shabbat?
Will Kurt blow out the candles?
Initiation *must* be more than dying.

JULY 4TH

You told me (by a costumed Morpheus
rolling in the splits) that you love me.
I swear in the reflection off your eyes
I saw myself swallow a red pill.

JULY 5TH

Spoonful of aged moroccon grind
and a mere 6 minutes later
You & I have our caffeeine in a cup
to water our bud

JULY 6TH

You know it's over

the moment you realize

their fatal flaw is

forever

JULY 7TH

If 28 has proven anything
I'll bet I can't win it back.
I'll stick with the penny slots
and free drinks from Brooklyn

JULY 8TH

Overlook your knighthood, your valor;
now is not the time for dragon slaying.
No one tells you you're living
in the best time of your life.

JULY 9TH

keep digging your moat,
build your towers tall,
get your glimpse of grand —
all castles become sand

JULY 10TH

while I was dreaming in the clouds
the birds on the branches above
plotted their revenge:
shit.

JULY 11TH

Could you drive a little slower?
I wanna take the long way
with you to anywhere but
home.

JULY 12TH

They'll return the favor if you
feed your demons.
Their cure for dark storms are
dark & stormies.

JULY 13TH

I'm not brave enough
to make you hate me.
Being loved by you
is painful enough.

JULY 14TH

glance at my watch
tap my toe
look up and look down and left and
right at the end

JULY 15TH

I'd like to think even
Thomas the Tank Engine
occasionally imagines
jumping in front of a train

JULY 16TH

A gravedigger walking
his dog at night
through a cemetery:
neither gets their relief.

JULY 17TH

Smile as wide as you want
when you whip out
your wallet:
your charity is not catharsis

JULY 18TH

The church bell rang
louder than anything
I'd heard before,
but silence is harder.

JULY 19TH

I, for one, welcome
any and all changes
that, for everyone,
decrease bad bowel movements

JULY 20TH

Mama told me the heart guides me
to where I want to give my life.
But the truth is
I haven't got a clue.

JULY 21ST

The stories we tell
to get the ending we want
is no secret, and yet
he had no secrets to reveal

JULY 22ND

Nurse your scars
back to freckled criss-cross
and no one not even you
will remember the score

JULY 23RD

the smartest souls i ever met
spend their time where
everybody's starving
but nobody's hungry

JULY 24TH

tick tick tick goes the universe.
tick tick tick goes the clock.
we're the ones who cock our guns
that make 'em go *tick tock*.

JULY 25TH

I saw you on the first day
of school get off another bus
and of course I yelled your name
like a fool

JULY 26TH

I knew it was you
when you stopped to fill the tank
and turned off the engine
before getting out to pump

JULY 27TH

Hold me
like your grudges,
until we forget how to
let go

JULY 28TH

Two sisters (following the form)
sat in the park
counting their fingers
like lyrics in a pop song

JULY 29TH

A case of mistaken serenity
left him defenseless,
like losing
a winning lottery ticket

JULY 30TH

I don't care for sunlight
when you're looking back at me.
Far on the horizon you stand,
eyes, an oasis.

JULY 31ST

We shared the past
but oh you know perhaps
we overshared.
(I wanted you so.)

AUGUST 1ST

now I understand why
you'd bite my lip when we kissed.
the weeklong black and blue is
how you marked your territory.

AUGUST 2ND

He was the best
spotlight operator
in the biz
with no following

AUGUST 3RD

He was fighting nature
He was fighting nurture
He regretted not sitting it out
and picking up the pieces

AUGUST 4TH

Whatever you do,
don't put a fan in your bedroom.
If you shit the bed
it'll hit the fan.

AUGUST 5TH

drown me
in burnt light roasts
so i can close my eyes
and finally see nothing

AUGUST 6TH

most legacies last
a few generations at most
but you can lengthen that
with the right seeds

AUGUST 7TH

They had this insane tradition
when you visited their castle.
They made you king and queen
but had you sit on the floor.

AUGUST 8TH

i'd rather you kill
my creations out of mercy
than let them starve to death,
wondering why they deserved it

AUGUST 9TH

rye whiskey and the smell of old books
smooth bodies with stronghold hooks
this romance of lifestyle
isn't as romantic as it looks

AUGUST 10TH

when all heads in concert nod
and monologues in unison echo
you're fooling yourself
(and not in the good way)

AUGUST 11TH

The city
with bridges can't seem to
connect with anyone
who isn't prototyping

AUGUST 12TH

Call me maestro.
The music's in the sheets,
and there's an orchestra
in my mouth

AUGUST 13TH

Easy, ready, willing, overtime
I'll do anything for the heart.
And although I don't believe in it
keep your hands off the soul

AUGUST 14TH

a bloody finger
a slice of skin
ungarnished glass
a cold flow on the move

AUGUST 15TH

She said it's better off in private.
(But she's only saying that because
she's not the one getting recognized
on the internet)

AUGUST 16TH

You have some nerve
telling me what new experiences
I must have.
There is only the chocolate Frosty.

AUGUST 17TH

A black Toyota Prius
gets T-boned at night
without running a red light.
The cops rule no driver at fault.

AUGUST 18TH

to you,

to you,

dear You,

to you.

AUGUST 19TH

stare at me
one more time.
(I'm sorry) you're still
not my type

AUGUST 20TH

"Protect me," pled your data.
"Hold our conversations in confidence,
only color yourself
when history is hiding."

AUGUST 21ST

Cut it out.
It's burned on my eyelids
ever since you left
your watermark

AUGUST 22ND

He grabbed a roll of paper towels,
got on his fucking hands and knees,
and cleaned up somebody else's mess.
Still would swipe left.

AUGUST 23RD

Moments travel faster than light.
You were so far away
I didn't realize your light went out
until it was too late

AUGUST 24TH

The crystal ball flickers and
the story arc snickers,
she tiptoes the streetlights
skipping stones across liquors

AUGUST 25TH

He went beyond unclenching.
He rested his hand open-faced upon his chest,
and only then did he see why
the hummingbird did not see him.

AUGUST 26TH

Took a shot and said,
"You have the kind of face
that looks better
after beer"

AUGUST 27TH

I've never wanted something
more than I
want you
to punch me back

AUGUST 28TH

It's a powerful thing.
Expectation is enough
to make you do
everything you hate.

AUGUST 29TH

His surging hunger forms
a prickly mouth that won't breathe
but itches so he scratches and scratches
the wounds that run blood down his neck

AUGUST 30TH

All the limelight ever wanted
was a shadow.
A dancing silhouette so precise
you'd swear it almost moved first.

AUGUST 31ST

They charmed the conference room
with a crooked smile
(and eyes that only whispered
in four letter words)

SEPTEMBER 1ST

She held a bag of unpopped popcorn,
an unremarkable bottle of red wine,
a shallow, nervous breath, and
the next 80 years

SEPTEMBER 2ND

She stutters at the dinner table
She ruins every plan
She wonders how her life's so stable —
She got that dope running man

SEPTEMBER 3RD

My best memories with you
were spent crammed in a room
ignoring the rest of the world,
forgetting

SEPTEMBER 4TH

they say showing up
is half the battle.
that's why i guarantee results
by not showing.

SEPTEMBER 5TH

the impossibility of
a single Home
is something no one wants
to accept

SEPTEMBER 6TH

Run toward your lighthouse and
sweat out the small stuff.
It's the little things
that add up to the garbage of life.

SEPTEMBER 7TH

She clutched my hand and told me
I was all she wanted,
that I was her white whale.
"You know he never catches it, right?"

SEPTEMBER 8TH

You're just a range
of longitudes and latitudes.
Cartography was never my forte,
and I'm sick of asking for directions.

SEPTEMBER 9TH

Somewhere in the farthest
corner of the universe
a distress signal is escalating
(We're more of a bug than a feature)

SEPTEMBER 10TH

The revolution of fire & salt:
an uprise, a downfall, a rift
over fault. Rinse & repeat:
the world's somersault.

SEPTEMBER 11TH

I'm looking for an escape artist.
Rise up on your mark to repel
down to sanctuary I'll get set take
your lead and drown you go first go.

SEPTEMBER 12TH

a nest is nothing
more than unnoble debris
unnecessarily mud-glued
together so we're together

SEPTEMBER 13TH

I've no want of roundtrip tickets
I've no time for green bananas
I've no gifts left to give only
steps to take & regrets to make

SEPTEMBER 14TH

the streets are kinder when you're
around the corner across the
road to reality sipping lemonade
cold you told me not in my backyard

SEPTEMBER 15TH

After long-enough darkness
sunshine is enough for frenzy.
I miss the madness.
I miss my mania.

SEPTEMBER 16TH

Among the pile of black and brown
there's a pair of red heels bright
enough to make Dorothy jealous.
"Who wears red heels to Auschwitz?"

SEPTEMBER 17TH

My life's museum is more pristine
than marble. Tourists and indigenous
huddle in masses holding tiny maps
hoping for a chance to leave

SEPTEMBER 18TH

The grass is greener here,
the sunshine sweeter here, but
my calendar can't seem to forget
your birthday

SEPTEMBER 19TH

A bottle of wine with an old "friend."
She fires her trigger-finger smile
and her what-if's & coulda-been's.
I see through you. I'm Neo dodging bullets.

SEPTEMBER 20TH

emerge not
from the dark night screaming
bloody murder
without a blade or motive

SEPTEMBER 21ST

My most intimate moment:
after a lovely evening in,
a post-saag-paneer dutch oven.
You're mine now.

SEPTEMBER 22ND

I hold with those who favor fire.
I crave the certain kind of crazy
that bites back (a bit).
I prefer my pasta al dente.

SEPTEMBER 23RD

You'll tell me I only sport a henley
because I saw some familiar face
wearing one in a magazine
but I really like it for me I think

SEPTEMBER 24TH

I could listen to
our chromatic scale all day,
but I can't make out if we're rising
or falling

SEPTEMBER 25TH

There's a fine line between being a romantic or serial killer. (I know I can be scary. I'm looking for someone to make a horror flick.)

SEPTEMBER 26TH

I wish I could mean this
I don't wish you peace (not right away)
May your civil war end the
way you need it to

SEPTEMBER 27TH

she was too blue for you
and unarguably too smart
(i pull you in tight demanding you
kiss me stupid)

SEPTEMBER 28TH

I said I'd make the same mistake
never again in a million years
But she can tell when I have to pee
and I still gallop down stairs

SEPTEMBER 29TH

someday somebody
will call me by my stage name
and that night my sleep will be so deep
I may make it my home

SEPTEMBER 30TH

the only way I know
how to stretch seconds out
leaves me left
and happy-sad for the week

AFTERWORD

Well, reader, what can I say? Everybody's raw writing hides tucked away in a drawer somewhere, and you came across mine and just read it all.

What started as a 30-day challenge became this project: every day, write a four line poem with no future revisions. Sharing them wasn't part of the plan, let alone publishing them unrevised, but I'm discovering that not caring about polish is as valuable as the act of creating itself.

So I'll be the first to admit that some of these poems are not good, and all of them (I mean *all* of them) are unheroic. But I like them as they are, and that's enough.

I still write a poem a day. Every couple weeks, I reread the most recent ones with an outsider's eye. I find beauty in the blemishes. I relish in the rough edges. It's as if I'm reading a diary of mine I don't remember writing.

Vonnegut said the "kick of creation is the act of creating, not anything that happens afterward," but what happens afterward? Reflection. He forgot to mention the kick of reflection.

Because if I'm being honest, these poems have become more than a ritual. They're a glimpse into my unconscious musings. An exhibit on self-therapy. A hurried response to existential dread—just trying to mend what's broken.

ACKNOWLEDGEMENTS

This book and its poems were inspired by the following:

The 27 Club, Aaron Faucher, Albert Camus, Alex, Anne Morrow Lindbergh, Averill Curdy, Ben Folds, Bethany Crystal, Blaine Billingsley, bill wurtz, Bogdan Haiducu, Charlie Kaufman, Chas Barton, Chester Bennington, Christy Spees, Chuck Norris, Daryl Hall & John Oates, Demi Lovato, e e cummings, Gabriel Blake, George R.R. Martin, Hayley Rose, hummus, Jed Feder, Jessica Pollack, Jenn Volk, Julia Gang, Katie Bock, Katrina Diaz, Kurt Vonnegut, Lin-Manuel Miranda, Lisa Kream, Mat Kearney, Meg Mac, Molly Babbington, Molly Collins, Mom (hi, Mom!), my therapist, The Northwestern University "Wildcat" Marching Band, Pasek and Paul, Phoebe Waller-Bridge, Poppy, Rachel Feder, Raghu and Meena Hariharan, Regina Spektor, Ria Mae, Robert Frost, Sara Bareilles, Sarah Kay, Sean Park, Sebastian DeLuca, Shaun Young, Steve Coleman, Tami Benchoam-Rogers, Taylor Mali, They Might Be Giants, The Wachowskis, Wendy's, The Wild Reeds, Will Borges, William Carlos Williams, Yad Vashem, and your name.

Thank you.

ABOUT THE AUTHOR

Born and raised near Chicago, Zack Moy has written tiny poems since he was eight years old. He currently lives in San Francisco where he's a recovering entrepreneur, software engineer, and executive producer. This is Zack's debut title. Learn more about him at zackmoy.com.

Made in the USA
San Bernardino, CA
03 March 2018